Celebrate Now!

35 Simple Ways to Bring Presence, Peace, and Happiness into Your Life

By Harmony Rose West

Other books in Soul-Full Self-Care
Series:
Calm Down!
Get Grounded!
Nurture Yourself!

Table of Contents

Introduction

When we feel jubilant or excited, our pathways of joy are turned on. These "joy pathways" have unusual names, such as the radiant circuits, strange flows, extraordinary vessels, and psychic channels. These channels of joy are often subdued by our stressful modern lifestyle since it is challenging to feel very joyful when you are overwhelmed and overloaded.

My husband and I were planning to move out of our home of twenty years, beginning to tackle the myriad of details needed to rent the house, as well as move into our new home. I was feeling a bit overwhelmed and not sure where to focus, when the phone rang. My husband's booming bass voice was on the other end of the line.

As I explained my overwhelm, he happily assured me, "Don't worry, be happy. We are on a grand adventure." His thoughtful, lively, positive communication engaged those radiant circuits and changed my state on the spot. I decided, right then and there, that I wasn't going to resist this transition. It was my choice and my choice alone how I was going to navigate our pending move.

It's your choice to tend to your joy. You owe it to yourself to spend a few minutes each day actively celebrating your life!

What is Soul-Full Self-Care?

Soul-Full Self-Care is about giving yourself small acts of kindness right now!   It's about **intentionally** focusing on tender acts of self-love.

Soul-Full Self-Care is not meant to be a one-shot fix. Self-care is most effective when applied in small but constant doses; a few minutes here and a few minutes there. They are sustainable, cumulative practices that calm the stress in your body while nurturing your spirit.

Soul-Full Self-Care uses the healing energy of your hands and your thoughts to strengthen you.

Soul-Full Self-Care rituals bring you back to the present moment, this precious now, where all of your power is. It's about being here, instead of there.

Soul-Full Self-Care is taking time to tend to your body, mind, heart, and spirit so you can walk strongly on your sacred life journey.

So, if you feel like you are galloping through your life, and you know you could use some **Soul-Full Self-Care**, you're in the right place. One act of **Soul-Full Self-Care** leads to another. Just take it one day at a time.

Blessings

1. Blessed Word of the Day

As I write now, I am listening to the album, "Feeling Good Today." Satnam Kaur and her children's choir are delightfully singing a song named "I am Blessed." I sing along and welcome the magical and peaceful tone these lyrics call into my day...

Today, the sun has risen and with it, the start of a new day. Today, you are able to savor its warmth. *Today, you are here.* With this new day comes a clean slate, if you choose to think of it that way. Yesterday has passed. Today is new. Tomorrow is yours to create.

Years ago, I read the book *If Not Now, When?* by Reverend Wayne Muller. In his book, he suggests that today might be your last day on the planet, so why not live as though it is? I have brought that idea into many of my days, and the influence has been profound. When I live a day as though it could be my last, I find I am more present, loving, and kind.

If you are reading this, you are blessed. You likely have plenty to eat, clothes on your back with many more in the closet, and a nice warm bed in a nice warm house. Not everyone is so blessed. It could do us all some good to remember that.

SOUL FULL self care

Choose a word that reflects your gratitude for yet another day, your gratitude for your blessings, and your gratitude for your life. Choose a word that will inspire you and guide you to live your day with purpose, like it's your last day on earth. Let this word become your *blessed word of the day*: blessed, peace, ease, friendship, love, caring, generosity... you get the idea. If it helps you to remember, write it down; write it on your calendar, leave a note on your bathroom mirror, set it as the background on your phone, do whatever you need to remind yourself. Having a *Blessed Word of the* Day is a sweet act of celebration.

~What can I do to always remember who I am ? Juan Ramon Jiminez~

2. Bless Money

How often do you worry about money? It seems to be an obsession with many of us. Years ago, some information came to me on the internet which changed my perspective about how rich I am. It's called "As the World Turns," and get ready for the shocking highlights:

If we were to shrink the earth's population to one village of 100 people, keeping existing human ratios remaining as they are now, 57 people would be Asian, 21 would be European, 14 would be from the North and South Hemisphere and eight would be African. About 52 of us would be female and 48 male. Roughly 30 of us would have white skin, the other 70 would not.

Okay, here's the shocking part:

80 people out of 100 would live in substandard housing.
70 would be unable to read.
50 would suffer from malnutrition.
One, and only one, would have a college education
One, and only one, would own a computer.
Six would possess all of the world's wealth, and all six people would be from....the United States.

If you have money in the bank, in your wallet, or spare change in a dish somewhere, you have more than 92% of the world's population! If you have food, clothes, a roof, and a place to sleep, you are richer than 75% of the rest of the world!

Does that change your perspective on your wealth? Does that make you want to be grateful for and celebrate all you have? Perspective is a wonderful way to calm ourselves down.

Whenever you spend money, whether you are writing a check, using your credit card or paying cash, stop, feel your feet anchored on the floor, and in your mind's eye declare, "I have more than enough money and plenty to share." Feel how soothing that feels. How wonderful would that be if that were the total truth?!

For years, I've been blessing my money, telling myself how rich I am. That doesn't mean that every single minute of every single day, I feel ridiculously rich. It does mean that anything we do is cumulative...whether it is being worried or grateful. I feel more and more ease around money, and that has to be a good thing.

~The real measure of your wealth is how much you'd be worth if you lost all your money. Author Unknown~

3. Bless You!

When you hear someone sneeze, your automatic response is to say "bless you." Looking into the dictionary, I've learned the power of our unique practice.

Definition of Blessing: *Something promoting or contributing to happiness, and the act of invoking divine protection or aid*

I like the idea that when I say "Bless you" I am invoking some really good energy that is going to support someone in the journey of their day. In her inspiring book, *The Dance*, Oriah Mountain Dreamer tells of leading a meditation during a writing retreat. She asked each person to sit in silence and write the truest statement possible about themselves.

After a minute or so, she picked up her pen to write her own statement: *I am blessed.* She knew immediately that this was the truest truth she could find. I think, deep down, we can all come to realize this truth about ourselves. *We are all blessed.*

SOUL FULL self care

Could saying "bless you" become a profound practice that could strengthen both you, me, and the world? Such a simple thing is worth a try.

Every time you hear anyone sneeze, declare out loud, "Bless you!" When you yourself sneeze, take a deep breath, place your hands over your heart and say "Bless you."

These two simple words, backed with purpose and intention, can contribute to happiness, and welcome divine protection into your life and the lives of others. Bless you. Bless me. Bless us all.

~If we perceived Life with reverence and understood our evolutionary process, we would stand in awe at the experience of physical life and walk the Earth in a very deep sense of gratitude. Gary Zukov~

BodyLove

4. Dry-Brush your Skin

Dry-brushing in the morning can wake you up better than "a cuppa joe," and it's way better for you than coffee! After a good dry-brushing, you will feel bright and bushy-tailed and ready to get moving into your day!

In addition to awakening and invigorating you, there are many other benefits, like removing dead skin cells and unclogging pores, which will leave your skin baby-butt soft. Dry-brushing increases circulation, so your skin will boast a healthy glow. It improves lymphatic drainage and reduces the appearance of cellulite.

Who wouldn't want all that?!

Dry-brushing, here we come!

SOUL FULL self care

Dry-brushing is simple. With a skin brush, use long, smooth strokes to brush your naked skin pretty much all over, going in towards your heart with each stroke. It's easiest to dry-brush right before your shower so the water can easily wash away the dry skin you've removed.

Tougher parts of your body, like your legs and feet, can be brushed firmly. Delicate areas like the inner thigh and neck should be brushed very gently, if at all. Use pressure that feels nice to you. The skin of the face is too delicate to brush with a dry body brush.

If you have a cut, abrasion, or rash on your skin, don't dry brush that area. Use common sense.

Almost everyone that has dry-brushed gets hooked! It's such an easy, inexpensive way to nurture and celebrate your body!

~Maybe that's why I want to touch people so often-it's only another way of talking. Georgia O'Keefe~

5. Spine Flex

Low back pain is a common health complaint of many adults. How many of us sit at the computer for hours on end? One of the best ways to avoid backaches is to keep your spine flexible so the cerebrospinal fluid is moving smoothly.

The yogis say that how youthful you feel is determined by the flexibility of your spine, so if you want to maintain a strong and healthy body, you need to maintain a flexible spine.

This exercise was taught to me by a friend who is a Kundalini yoga teacher. It is a really powerful way to strengthen your spine and wake your whole body up!

Find a comfortable place to sit, either cross-legged on the floor, or while sitting in a chair.

Slow your breathing down.
Grab your ankles and as you inhale, powerfully, flex your spine forward, keeping your shoulders relaxed, and your head straight.

Exhale and relax your spine back to its original position.

Continue breathing deeply as you rhythmically move your spine back and forth. With each inhalation, feel the energy going down your spine. With each exhalation, feel your breath coming back up your spine. See if you can feel energy in your third eye, the space between your eyebrows. Do this exercise for a few minutes.
Bring this flexibility into celebrating the rest of your day!

~Self-discipline is when your conscience tells you to do something and you don't talk back. W. K. Hope~

6. Whoo Hoo Shampoo!

My mother was a hairdresser, and she gave me the best shampoos! As a young girl, I remember begging her to wash my hair, oohing and ahhing through the head massage. She never, ever shampooed my head long enough!

Over the years, since my mother no longer lives with me, I've learned to shampoo my own head! Of course, when I began, I was just washing my hair but knew, thanks to my mother, that hair washing was just an excuse to experience an awesome head massage. I feel the tension in my head lessening with just a bit of rubbing.

As time passed, I learned that I could "dry shampoo" my hair as well as shampoo as I ordinarily do. I omit the water and shampoo and just massage my head. It feels sooo good...I feel my intuition sharpen, my senses clear, and I feel awake, inspired and celebrated. Life feels good.

SOUL FULL self care

When you are taking a shower or bath, shampoo your head with gusto! Suds your hair up and rock and roll those fingers on that cranium...doesn't that feel great? Anytime during the day that your head feels congested, give yourself a "dry shampoo." Scrub those troubles away! Make room in your head!

Be forewarned that if anyone sees you, they will longingly wish you that you would massage their head too!

~I've learned that no matter what happens or how bad it seems today, life does go on, and it will be better tomorrow.
Maya Angelou~

Energy Medicine

7. Four Memory Pumps

How many times do you walk into a room only to forget why you are there?! Most likely, you have too much on your plate to remember every single detail of your life. Yet, when you walk into a room, it's nice to be able to remember why you are there! One deep way to celebrate your life is to do whatever you can to keep your memory sharp and clear.

This "Four Memory Pumps" exercise improves the flow of cerebrospinal fluid which will help you think more clearly. Oxygen-rich cerebrospinal fluid gets drawn up the spine, which supports the nervous system while delivering precious nutrients to your brain.

SOUL FULL self care

Place the palm of your left hand on the left side of your head with your fingers crossing over the top of your head. Place your right hand in the middle of your chest. Take three deep breaths, breathing in through your nose like you are smelling a rose, and breathing out like you are blowing out a candle.

Keep you right hand on your chest, and move your left hand so that your palm is on your forehead and your fingers are stretched over the top of your head. Take three more deep breaths.

Move your left hand onto your chest. Place your right hand to the right side of your head and take three deep breaths.

Keep your left hand on your chest. Place the palm of your right hand on the back of your head and take three deep breaths.

~Asleep too long, we need to wake. Awake too long, we need to sleep.
Author Unknown~

8. Got Energy?

We are energy beings. There is energy inside us, outside us and all around us. Albert Einstein, one of the most intelligent humans that ever lived, taught us that everything is energy. "Okay, everything might be energy", you may exclaim, "but I don't feel it." Well if you can't feel energy, how do you know it is real? As with learning anything, practice is the key. If you want to feel energy, you need to practice feeling energy.

Years ago, I read about John Holt learning to play the cello. This is what he said:

> Not many years ago, I began to play the cello. Most people would say that what I am doing is "learning to play" the cello. But these words carry into our minds the strange idea that there exists two very different processes.
>
> 1. Learning to play the cell, and 2. Playing the cello
>
> They imply that I will do the first until I have completed it, at which point, I will stop the first process and begin the second. In short, I will go on "learning to play" until I have "learned to play" and then "I will begin to play." Of course, this is nonsense. There are not two processes but one. We learn to do something by doing it. There is no other way.

Feeling energy is just like that. You learn how to feel energy by doing it. There is no other way.

SOUL FULL self care

Rub your two hands together and shake them off. Rub them together again, quite briskly. Now, hold your palms facing together, and feel the energy between them. Pull your hands slowly apart, rounding your palms so that you are holding an energy ball. Feel the energy between your hands. If you aren't sure that you are feeling energy, try it again and again and again. You will learn how to feel energy by feeling energy over and over again. There is no other way. Celebrate being a learner.

~We struggle to find life outside ourselves, unaware that the life we are seeking lies within. Kahlil Gibran~

9. Heaven Rushing In

Oh, the wonder of a brand new day...of a brand new hour...of a brand new moment!
We get so embroiled in our thoughts and doings that we aren't often conscious of the beauty and mystery of celebrating the wonder of the present moment.

As I get older, I am getting better at reveling in the magnanimousness of each day. My children have grown into adults, my grandchildren are growing like weeds, I've lost my two dearest friends to cancer and many more to the inevitable effects of aging. These "awarenesses" help me remember that I am blessed to be alive and to not take all of my days for granted.

Each day is a precious gift. That's why it's called the present.

SOUL FULL self care

This energy exercise will become one of your favorites.
Everyone always feels more grateful and connected to
the creative energies of the universe after doing *Heaven
Rushing In*.

Stand and ground yourself with your hands on your
thighs. Throughout this exercise, breathe in through
your nose like you're smelling a rose and breathe out like
you're blowing out a candle. Bring your hands together in
a prayerful position at the center of your chest.

Raise both hands and arms up and open them wide as you
breathe deeply and symbolically welcome and embrace
the energy of the heavens. Feel the energy of this day
pouring into your heart space. Welcome in miracles,
synchronicities, people, places, and things that are for
your highest good. Gather this healing energy and ground
it into your heart chakra in the middle of your chest.

*~If you knew who walked beside you on this path you have
chosen, you would never feel fear or doubt again. The Course
in Miracles~*

10. Butt in the Air!

Your capacity for happiness and joy is hard-wired into your body, mind, and spirit. Joy is carried along a network known as the Radiant Circuits, strange flows, or in Traditional Chinese Medicine, extraordinary vessels. Donna Eden, author of *Energy Medicine* describes them as hyperlinks as on the web, jumping to wherever they are needed (which is why the Chinese found them to be both extraordinary and strange.)

These radiant energies are critical for maintaining your health and well-being. They have the essential task of connecting and harmonizing all your energy systems. Because of the stress of modern-day living, these energies often struggle to stay front and center in your life. If your radiant circuits are not flowing, you just can't feel as much joy as is your birthright.

If depression or negativity are persistent themes in your life, if you are caught in the past from earlier traumas, if certain habits of thought or behavior are resistant to change, then you may need to activate your radiant circuits.
One of the easiest ways to activate these circuits is to do this hysterically funny-sounding exercise called Butt in the Air!

SOUL FULL self care

You've seen how babies stick their butts in the air?! We are gonna do just that! Kneel down on all fours, with your knees on the floor. Push back so that your butt is resting on your heels and bring your hands to your sides as you gently lower your head to the ground. Raise your butt into the air as high as you can comfortably go. Hold this position for two to three minutes. Why not use this time to think of something uplifting and celebrate your life?

~People are like stained-glass windows. They sparkle and shine when the sun is out, but when the darkness sets in, their true beauty is revealed only if there is a light from within.
Elizabeth Kübler-Ross~

11.   Drink Water Mindfully

Dr. Emoto is a Japanese scientist made famous with his experiments with water. In a nutshell, Emoto and other scientists sang, spoke to, and wrote messages on glasses of water. They then froze the water and studied the resulting water crystals. Some of the messages the scientists spoke were beautiful, such as "thank you," and "I love you." They spoke messages of peace, and played classical music. Other communications to the water were negative, such as "I hate you," and "get out of my way," and they played heavy metal music.

Always, the water responded to their input. Always the water formed amazing and unique crystalline structures. Their uplifting messages created beautiful water crystals, while mean communications created strange, unpleasant shapes. Check out Emoto's book, *Messages in Water.* Dr. Emoto proved that our interactions with water are really meaningful.

After I visited a village in Ecuador where I witnessed young children outside laundering their own clothing, with unclean water, I decided to anchor Emoto's messages more into my own life.

We in the western world take our relatively clean water for granted. We are blessed to have an abundance of water pouring right out of our faucets. Since gratitude is such a powerful medicine, I began thanking the water that comes out of my tap, trusting that it would bring some good mojo to it. I began blessing the water I drink, cook with, bathe in, and use for laundry. Thank you, thank you, thank you, dear water. A daily practice unfolded of thanking the water in my body, believing and trusting that this simple ritual would strengthen me.

At home or work, find a special glass to drink your water out of. If you are drinking out of a water bottle, tie a ribbon around the neck of it.

This special glass or ribbon becomes an anchor that helps you remember you are learning something new. You are teaching yourself a new habit of being thankful for the water you drink. Every time you take a sip of your water, say thank you to yourself.

Thank you, throat, for being able to swallow. Thank you, earth, for this amazing liquid. Thank you for having a mind that is open to learning. Thank you for anchoring me in this present moment. Thank you for this clean, fresh water. Thank you, thank you, thank you. May these drops of gratitude moisten and celebrate the precious moments of my life.

~There are two ways to live your life. One is as though nothing is a miracle. The other is as though everything is a miracle. Albert Einstein~

12.   Namaste

The declaration of the word 'Namaste' is the customary greeting that begins and often ends conversations between two East Indian people.

In Sanskrit, the word *namah* means "I bow to you. I extend my greetings and salutations to you." This beautiful greeting has the spiritual significance of reducing one's ego in the presence of another.

There is even more to this beautiful custom. The true meeting between people is the meeting of their minds. In a deeper sense, when we greet one another using the Namaste greeting, it means, "may our minds meet," indicated by the folded palms placed in front of the chest. The bowing down of the head is an ego-less way of extending friendship with love, respect, and humility.

Namaste has a deep spiritual significance, recognizing that the life force, the divinity, the Self, or the God in me is the same in you and in all beings.

As you bring your hands together and bow slightly, you honor and celebrate the Divinity in the person before you.

SOUL FULL self care

Practice the Namaste greeting with at least one person today.
Gracefully and easily, bring your palms together in a prayerful position in front of your chest.

As you speak Namaste, bow your head slightly in reverence to the one before you.
Feel how connected you are to this person and to all beings.
Namaste!

~In seeking what is essential, we become essential. Author Unknown~

13.   Waterfall of Appreciation

Many years ago, when I was first beginning to facilitate women's circles, I had the best idea ever! I had learned an idea called a Rampage of Appreciation from Abraham-Hicks. Basically, it's an active exercise of quickly saying, out loud, a long string of things you are grateful for.

We sat in a circle around a giant glass bowl and each woman was given a string of semi-precious stones beads...amethyst, citrine, malachite, garnet, smoky, and clear quartz. I instructed every woman to toss a bead into the bowl while she uttered one thing in her life she was grateful for.

Six women armed with six strands of beads, produced the most amazing sounds. Woman sang the praises of their lives as they tossed beads into the bowl, and the bowl reverberated with the joy of the moment with an amazing song. A singing bowl of gratitude! We followed this soothing, yet electrifying experience by stringing the beads into a bracelet. Each woman brought home a tender treasure to wear as a reminder of her blessings. I still treasure my Waterfall of Appreciation celebration bracelet.

SOUL FULL self care

Sit for a moment with your eyes closed. Take some deep breaths, and feel your body sitting on the chair. Bring yourself more and more present. Feel how blessed you are, right here, right now.

Out loud, begin your Waterfall of Appreciation…"thank you lips for all the kisses you give…thank you feet for all the steps you take…thank you bed for a warm, soft place to rest…thank you trees for all the oxygen you provide"…and keep going. Celebrate your abundance!

~Appreciate yourself and express gratitude for the richness of your life. Your children will naturally follow your example. Harmony Rose West~

HeartWork

14.   Nine Hearts

The energies of joy have an entire energetic system all their own and are aptly called the Radiant Circuits. You know when they are activated, because you feel a thrill of happiness. When you see an amazing sunset, feel love, or hold a puppy or kitten, your Radiant Circuits are engaged. Sadly, too often, in your stress-filled, fast-paced life, your Radiant Circuits sink down into a state of inactivity and become dormant. You will feel happier and healthier if you make time to laugh and play and feel the joy of being alive.

If you ask anyone from anywhere in the world to draw a picture of love or joy, everyone is sure to include the same image. That image is a heart, the symbol for love and for the Radiant Circuits. Let's intentionally activate the Radiant Circuits with the Nine Hearts energy exercise

SOUL FULL self care

This exercise is usually done while standing, though it is beneficial whether you are standing, sitting, or lying down.

With both hands, trace three hearts on your face beginning at the chin, going up to the hairline, down the temples and cheeks making the point of the heart at the chin. Inhale as you trace the beginning of the heart up the center of your face, and exhale as you trace the second half of the heart down to your chin.

Move your hands to the middle of your chest, and trace three hearts over your chest. Go up and around your breasts, making the point of the heart at the pubic bone area. Inhale as you trace the beginning of the heart up the center of your chest and exhale as you trace the second half of the heart down to your navel.

Finish by tracing three large hearts from your toes up the center of your body to over your head and around your whole body. Inhale as you trace the beginning of the heart up in the inside of your legs and exhale as you trace the second half of the heart down the outside of your legs to your feet. Feel and celebrate the LOVE!

~Don't ask what the world needs. Ask what makes you come alive and go do it. Because what the world needs is people who have come alive. Howard Thurman~

15.   Read Inspiration

I've made a conscious choice not to read the daily
newspaper. There's just too much bad news in those
tabloids. I remember when I used to read them, that my
breathing would get shallow, and often I would feel
discouraged or disgusted.
I would bet money that there's just as many good things
happening in the world. It's unfortunate that most of
them don't show up in the daily paper.

A friend of mine sent me a subscription to The Funny
Times. The content in there brings belly laughs! If you
are going to read the newspaper, maybe the comics
should be your focus!

SOUL FULL self care

Put the newspapers aside. Instead, begin your day by reading something uplifting...The Book of Awakening, The Course in Miracles, The Bible, The Koran, a book of poetry.

If you have a few moments to spare during the day, read a page from something that inspires you, something to help you celebrate your connection to your own divinity.

~Burn cooler and more efficiently, live longer. Marcia Wieder~

16.   Reach Out and Touch Someone

Are you aware of the benefits of oxytocin? Referred to as the love or trust hormone, oxytocin is being touted as a crucial brain chemical that helps keep psychological and physiological problems at bay. One of the best things to know about oxytocin is that you can get an easy fix anywhere at any time. All you need to do is simply touch someone! The simple act of touching bare skin causes your brain to release low levels of oxytocin -- both in you AND the person you are touching! More good news is that this effect lingers after the contact. It is said that oxytocin levels rise when you gaze at someone you love, so start staring at those you care about!

Offering a compliment to someone increases your level of oxytocin. Receiving a compliment also increases this hormone. What is even more outrageous is that hearing someone compliment someone else will raise YOUR oxytocin level! How amazingly great is that?!

My daughter and I used to play a silly game. I would touch her and say "thank you" for something she did. She would touch me as she said "thank you for thanking me" to which I would touch her and respond "thank you for thanking me for thanking you." We would continue our touchy-feely thank-you game until we would be laughing at the pure silliness of it. Oxytocin Heaven!

SOUL FULL self care

Today, reach out and touch someone as you thank him or her for something. Remember the touching part is important. You only need to touch his or her bare hand as you say thank you. You will elevate her oxytocin, your oxytocin, and perhaps that of someone who is watching your interaction.

~The eyes experience less stress when they look upon a wider horizon. R. D. Chin~

17.   Inner Light

There is a divine spark of creation within each and every one, that
some call their Inner Light. It's that special, yet paradoxically commonplace, brilliance in each human. Though invisible, this essential, non-physical part of us is the eternal flame that radiates from beyond the material realm.

Why not celebrate your own unique piece of the mystery of life? No one else is exactly like you. You are as unique as a snowflake, and just like each snowflake is necessary to make a cold snowbank, you are a unique, creative, totally-needed part of humanity. You have talents, gifts, and abilities that are uniquely yours. Humanity needs you to share them with all of us

SOUL FULL self care

Wear a necklace that has a special meaning for you, preferably one that comes in contact with your heart. Wear this necklace to symbolize a traditional "medicine bundle" worn by shamans to hold their personal power objects.

Your "medicine bundle" is metaphorically housed in your heart. Your bundle holds your everyday power objects of love, understanding, patience, belief, kindness, and wisdom. It houses all the gifts, talents, and abilities that are uniquely yours.

Each time you touch your necklace, take a deep breath, and celebrate the sacred powerful medicines that live within you.

~I tried so hard to please that I never realized no one is watching. Author Unknown~

Intention

18.   Every Day in Every Way

Autobiography in Five Chapters by Portila Nelson:

Chapter 1. I walk down the street. There is a deep hole in the sidewalk.
I fall in. I am lost. I am hopeless. It isn't my fault. It takes forever to find a way out.

Chapter 2. I walk down the street and pretend I don't see the hole in the sidewalk. I fall in again. I can't believe I am in the same place but, it isn't my fault. It still takes a long time to get out.

Chapter 3. I walk down the same street. There is a deep hole in the sidewalk.
I see it is there. I fall in. It's a habit. My eyes are open. I know where I am. It is my fault. I get out immediately.

Chapter 4. I walk down the same street. There is a deep hole in the sidewalk. I walk around it.

Chapter 5. I walk down another street.

How many times have you found yourself walking down the same street, filled with holes, and it doesn't even occur to you to take a different route? How many times have you thought the same thought, and it doesn't occur to you to interrupt that pattern? We need skills to help us think stronger thoughts.

Emile Coue, a medical hypnotist who lived in the 1920's, had amazing results helping people break stubborn patterns. He taught them to daily mechanically repeat this phrase twenty times, "Every day, in every respect, I am getting better and better." In order to have this auto-suggestion be effective, he counseled, eliminate the will completely and only engage your imagination.

SOUL FULL self care

Take a piece of string and tie 20 knots on the string, or use a string of beads or mala beads. When you wake up, lie in bed, or sit up and close your eyes. Now, hold the string and touching one knot at a time, repeat this Couism in a monotonous manner, while **moving your lips** (this is important), 'Every day in every way, I am getting better and better. Every day in every way, I am getting better and better." There is no need to think of anything in particular.

When you eat food, you don't need to tell the food to go to your little toe. The same is true with this mantra - - it will go where it is needed. All you need to add is trust. It may help you walk down another street in your mind.

~At the moment you are most in awe of all there is about life that you don't understand, you are closer to understanding it all than at any other time. Jane Wagoner~

19.   Elevated Octaves

Following the guidance of channel Paul Selig, I closed my eyes and intended that with every inhale, I would raise my vibration one octave. I wasn't sure what raising an octave would feel like, but it seemed a worthy use of my time!

Inhaling, I imagined my breath had the capacity to infuse my aura with light and love. Exhaling, I intentionally decided to release any beliefs or ideas that stood in my way. Ten intentional breaths. Inhaling love and light. Exhaling any resistance. I felt my energy expanding as it was nurtured by this focused consciousness.

The change in my state was palpable. Three minutes of bringing my awareness into present time in this unusual way strengthened my body, mind, heart, and soul. I felt like my energy took up space in a very sweet way. As I re-entered my day, I imagined, sensed, and perceived that I was a bright bubble of healing light sending healing energy to all I came into contact with.

SOUL FULL self care

Find a place to comfortably sit. If possible, have your feet planted on the earth. If you are inside, imagine your feet connected to the earth.

You are going to take ten very intentional inhalations and exhalations. One, inhaling and calling to the light within you. Exhaling, letting go of any beliefs you have that you can't access this energy or that this will be hard or kooky.

Two, inhaling, infuse your body with light and love, trusting that with each breath, the feeling will grow and be more palpable to your physical senses. Two, exhaling, letting go of anything that feels like stress or resistance. Do this for ten waves of breathing, then sit still for a moment and feel your elevated vibration. Bring this celebrating energy into your day.

~The most precious gift we can offer is our presence. When mindfulness embraces those we love, they will bloom like flowers. Thich nat Hanh~

20.   A Brand New Day

It happened again!

Magically and effortlessly the sun rose in the sky. Birds are singing sweet notes of awakening and celebration. The buzz of the day's activities begins anew. Yesterday is gone forever. Today is a totally new beginning. Life unfolds.

Whatever challenges yesterday presented are over. Today presents an opportunity to start again, amend, and create anew.

Welcome this brand new day. It marks the present; a gift to be treasured. Tomorrow, this day too will be a part of the past.

SOUL FULL self care

Stand outside and mindfully salute the sun as you express gratitude for this brand new day. Feel the strength of the sun as you breathe deeply into your solar plexus and hold the sun's warmth there.

As you feel the warmth in your belly, imagine a hot air balloon floating overhead containing all the possibilities of this brand new day. Feel the blessings of all the opportunities that are out there and represented by this balloon effortlessly floating over your head.

Breathe these blessings into your heart.

Make a decision to walk consciously through this day as you celebrate its wonder.

~In order for our minds to grow and to become as expansive as the universe, we first need to cultivate the attitude of a small child. Amma~

21.   Forgetting Everything is All Right

A Course in Miracles teaches that we either live in Love or Fear. Our world is deeply entrenched in a matrix of FEAR. The newspapers are overflowing with fear-based news. Advertisements are based in fear also. Buy this widget and you will be enough. Something is wrong with you as you are...you need this to be complete.

I once heard an acronym for FEAR described as *False Evidence Appearing Real*. A friend of mine says FEAR means *F--- Everything and Run!* I now believe that when we are in FEAR, it means we are *Forgetting Everything is All Right*. We are exactly who we are supposed to be and becoming who we choose to be. Everything is All Right.

Everything is All Right. You have a roof over your head. You have plenty of food. Slow down and feel that everything is all right. Decelerate your pace so you can love and appreciate your life. Love and appreciate yourself. You don't have forever. This is it. Do you want to live in love or fear? Do you want to appreciate yourself or fear that you're not enough?

SOUL FULL self care

Stand in front of the bathroom mirror, or better yet, find a hand mirror and sit yourself down. Take a few deep breaths and feel your breath going in and out of your nose. Feel your feet planted on the floor as you feel yourself slow down. This will just take a few minutes.

Look at yourself in the mirror, not in the usual way you do, picking pimples and fixing your hair. Instead, focus on your eyes as you make eye contact with your spirit.

Keep breathing as you stare into your own eyes. Your eyes are the windows of your soul. You are making deep contact with your essence.

Stay here for a few moments. Breathe. Tell yourself that everything is all right. Consciously choose to let go of any fear that you are not enough. Choose to feel love for yourself, for the soul that you are. You are wonderful. Your body is a great vehicle for your spirit.

When you are finished, close your eyes and feel this love. Bring this connection with yourself into your day.

~The privilege of a lifetime is being who you are. Joseph Campbell~

Joy

22.   Laughing all the Way

Remember how hard you used to laugh when you were a child? It's been said that children laugh 300 times a day, while we adults laugh 20 times a day. That sad statistic needs to change now!

Health-care professionals tell us that laughing helps lower blood pressure, and boosts immune function while reducing stress. Laughing also triggers the release of endorphins, the body's natural painkillers. A good belly laugh exercises the diaphragm, relaxes muscles and gives your heart a good workout.   Laughter has no known side effects (unless you count laughing until your belly hurts or you cry!)

Life can be stressful and good mental health, which includes a sense of humor, allows us to cope with sources of conflict and distress. For all of us, laughter can help change a mood, enhance a learning situation, and build us into stronger, healthier people.

Laughing helps bring a lighter perspective to life's challenges. A few chuckles can bring relief from strong emotions like guilt, anger, and fear. This free medicine helps us create a calmer sense of well-being. No wonder we have all heard that laughter is the best medicine. Laughter should be a necessary part of every single day, for both adults and children.

SOUL FULL self care

You felt it coming, didn't you?! Don't resist! When you are feeling like you need a change of perspective, an energy pick-up, a reason to feel happy just because...laugh! You can be sitting at your computer, stopped at a red light, about to lose it with your kids....Stop and take a deep breath and....LAUGH...laugh for a whole minute (you'll get to feel how long a minute can be!) Really, why not?! What have you got to lose except your stressful bad mood?

A mother was telling her little girl what her own childhood was like: "We used to skate outside on a pond. I had a swing made from a tire; it hung from a tree in our front yard. We rode our pony. We picked wild raspberries in the woods." The little girl was wide-eyed, taking all this in. At last she said, "I sure wished I'd gotten to know you sooner!"

23.   Smiling is Infectious

We are naturally drawn to people who smile. A smiling person seems to bring happiness with them. They seem to light up a room. Just observing someone who is smiling can change your mood. Stress can really show up in our faces. Smiling helps us from looking tired, worn down, and overwhelmed. The muscles we use to smile lift the face, making us look younger. Maybe smiling could be the next natural facelift!

Did you know that when you smile, there is a measurable reduction in your blood pressure? A study was done with those who had a blood pressure monitor at home. They sat for a few minutes, took a reading, then smiled for one minute and took another reading. Yup, just from smiling, they noticed a measurable difference in their blood pressure. Smiling is a natural drug!

I was shocked to learn that smiling has the same mood-boosting effect as eating 2000 bars of chocolate or being given a lot of money (just how is that measured!?)

Smiling is infectious. You catch it like the flu.
When someone smiled at me today, I started smiling too.
I passed around the corner and someone saw my grin.
When he smiled, I realized I'd passed it on to him.
I thought about that smile then I realized its worth.
A single smile, just like mine, could travel round the earth.
So if you feel a smile begin, don't leave it undetected.
Let's start an epidemic quick and get the whole wide world infected! Author Unknown

SOUL FULL self care

Take a break from whatever you are doing, and turn up the corner of those lips. Smile for one minute, and feel how it changes your state of mind. Smile as you go back to whatever you were doing.

~Smile. It only takes thirteen muscles. A frown takes sixty-four. Author Unknown~

24.   Tapping in the Joy

You can easily and intentionally tap the spirit of joy into your nervous system, which helps release stress and anchor in present moment goodness.

Tapping on your third eye assists you in anchoring and imprinting positivity into your nervous system. It is very powerful to tap on this place as you recall or experience sensations of joy, gratitude, a laugh, or even a sweet thought.

Don't let the simplicity of this exercise fool you! Tapping creates a rhythmic pulse of affirmative energy. Your body is used to your heartbeat, so tapping feels comforting and life-giving.

Lightly tapping on the third eye point while you feel joy pulses the joy throughout your nervous system, teaching it to be able to hold onto more and more joy.

SOUL FULL self care

When you are feeling joy, love, or gratitude in your life, tap this goodness in at your third eye, which is the space between your two eyebrows, above the bridge of your nose.

Tap with the middle finger of either hand for five to 10 seconds as you breathe deeply. Celebrate your good feelings permeating into your nervous system, anchoring in this positivity.

~Practice excellence. Avoid perfection. Practice acceptance.
Avoid resistance.
Author Unknown~

25.   My Body is Love

Chances are that your body doesn't look like you want it to: it's too fat, too wrinkly, too old, too grey, too thin, your butt is too big, your breasts are too small. Yet you still can give your one and only body some love. After all, it has carried your spirit around all these years. It deserves some kindness and compassion!

A friend recently celebrated her 40th birthday and talked of a realization she'd had. "I saw a photo of myself when I was 20 and I looked pretty dang good." she said, "But I didn't think I looked good then. I was too critical of myself. You know I still am critical of my body. But when I am 80 and I look at a photo of myself now when I'm 40, I am going to think I looked pretty good. So why wait?! I might as well appreciate myself now instead of waiting until I'm 80. That time may never come."

We should all take her realization to heart. It's a good way to go...love and celebrate yourself now...why wait? You don't know how much time you have left.

SOUL FULL self care

Take a moment and stand in front of the mirror. A good time to do this is after you take a shower. I know you don't want to do this...but do it anyway!
Take a good look at your body and appreciate it. Love it just the way it is.

Notice your hair, your face, your breasts, your belly, your legs. Take it all in. Love your body just as it is. Loving it doesn't mean that you don't want it to change. Change is good.

Loving your body means that you don't restrict self-love because your body isn't as perfect as you might like. No one's is! Love and celebrate your body no matter what.
It will make it easier to change whatever you are critical of.

~If I had a prayer, it would be this: God spare me from the desire for love, approval, and appreciation. Amen. Byron Katie~

26. Spontaneous Celebration

Free from adult responsibilities, children are naturally joyful much of the time. Maybe you've forgotten that as a child you were freer and perhaps more joyful. I can almost hear you say, 'I'd be joyful now too if I didn't have all these responsibilities!"

Unlike us, children don't lug around the past or contemplate the future.
Children are present-tense critters; they occupy the present; right here, right now. Left to themselves, they are quite content with the present moment.

In our perpetual state of busyness, we can often overlook this natural state of contentment. Children have a lot to teach us!

SOUL FULL self care

Have a spontaneous celebration of life!

Pull out a birthday candle and put it smack dab in the middle of your pancake, cornbread, or whatever else you are eating. If you are a parent, look into your child's surprised face as you light the candle.

Decide that even if this seems silly, life is to be celebrated. and you are celebrating, right here, right now! Feel the power of deciding to celebrate the present moment. Remember that this day is a gift. That's why they call it the present!

~There are a thousand ways to kneel and kiss the ground. Rumi~

Meditation

27.   Healing Light Meditation

SOUL FULL self care

Sit comfortably, close your eyes, and center yourself. Feel your bottom on your chair, your feet on the floor. Let the inhaling and exhaling of your breath bring your attention to this very moment. Feel your chest expanding and relaxing. Imagine, sense, and perceive a ball of white light sitting on the top of your head. Decide that light has the healing power to calm you while simultaneously energizing you.

The light is yummy and warm and as you exhale. It flows like melted white chocolate right down into your head. Let it relax all the muscles of your face, including your jaw and your eyes. This white light flows down into your neck and your shoulders, melting all the tension that you carry there.

This light fills your chest and your belly, all the way to the back of you, melting any tension that might be there. Allow this light to flow down into your arms and out your fingers.

With every exhalation, you find yourself surrendering to this healing ball of light. You feel it flowing into your hips, down your thighs, bathing your knees and legs and feet and out your toes. Feel gratitude and celebration for this light, allowing it to melt away anything unlike itself.

Take as much time as you choose...one minute or a few minutes. Bring this sense of lightness into the rest of your day.

~I have a dream. Martin Luther King~

Sit comfortably with your spine straight and arms and legs uncrossed. Feel your feet on the floor. Close your eyes as you bring your awareness to your breath as you feel how effortless it is to breathe.

Now sense a glowing ball of light in the center of your chest as you breathe deeply into your heart center.

Feel appreciation for someone, somewhere, or something. Imagine your children or grandchildren, a place in nature, or an image of something that brings you happiness. Let your breathing bring you deeper into this space of appreciation. Stay with this beautiful sense of appreciation for as long as you choose.

Appreciating in this way brings feelings of peace, and an experience that the present moment is enough.

Bring this sacred sense of spaciousness and appreciation with you into your day.

Buddha was asked, "What have you gained from meditation?" "I've gained nothing" replied Buddha. "But let me tell you what I lost - anger, anxiety, depression, insecurity, fear of old age, and death."

SOUL FULL self care

Sit in a quiet place where you won't be disturbed. Get yourself comfortable and close your eyes. Tune into your breathing. Take a few moments to slow yourself down letting your breath be your guide. When you are breathing slow and easy, you are ready to begin.

Imagine, sense, and perceive that there is a teeny, tiny speck of light in your heart space. As you tune into it, you can feel the spark of light, you can see this spark. It might even have a hum to it. Stay with whatever sensations you find yourself having.

Let this golden light grow from a tiny spark to a small flame. Fan it with your awareness and watch as it grows. It flickers beautiful golden light. The light feels so good. This beautiful light shines brilliantly, filling your heart with its subtle warmth.

This tender fire glowing in your heart represents your self-worth. It symbolizes your worth as a Divine being on the planet at this moment in time. There's no need to judge, no figuring anything out, no needing to do or think.

You feel content in the knowing of yourself as a worthy spark of the Divine. You embrace and embody your worth, and when you are ready, you open your eyes and carry this celebratory knowing into your day. Namaste.

Movement

30.   Dance to Infinity

While hovering or in flight, a hummingbird's wings dance in a repeating figure-eight pattern. This wing beat is a sacred symbol of infinity, the never-ending expansion of the universe.

This dance showcases the balance of the masculine and feminine through a constant movement of giving and receiving. The fluid center of the symbol reminds us of our own need to give and receive.

SOUL FULL self care

Put on music you love, music you can feel, music that makes you want to move!
Start to dance, creating large figure eights with your arms.

Experiment with holding both palms face up – a gesture of receiving, alternating with both your palms face down – a gesture of giving.

Continue to dance to infinity until the end of your song. Bring this newfound celebration of giving and receiving into the rest of your day.

~When was the last time you danced?
Question put to the sick by a Native American Medicine Man~

31.   Dance with the Birds

My adorable two-year-old granddaughter, Lyla Rain, and I had bath time while we toddler-talked about noses, ears, and little toes. Afterwards, we took pails full of tub water out to water the garden. As I conservatively watered, Lyla was splashing the water everywhere.

Suddenly a flock of Pinyon jays flew right over our heads. As it passed, Lyla spontaneously began cooing and cawing and screeching. Whether she was imitating their song or calling to them, I'm not sure.

Her sounds were loud and uninhibited. As her wide-eyed cherubic face lit up like the rays of the sun, she danced around -- celebrating her experience of the flight of the flock. Unselfconsciously and exuberantly she sang her elation. Energetically, I could feel her become one with the birds, and I swear I wouldn't have been surprised if she sprouted wings, spread them out, and took flight.

I was moved to tears by her presence and by her immediate declaration of delight of that which was happening in the here and now. Even her water play took second place.

As she looked to me, still flapping her little arms, I could hear her wonder, "Why aren't you singing and dancing, Nana?" *Right then and there, I became aware of how adult I am. Did I ever have that exuberation? I'm not sure, but I sure want it now, don't you?*

SOUL FULL self care

Find some music that you enjoy, put it on loud, even louder!... and dance. Dance like there is nothing to do, nowhere to go. Dance like this is the last and only opportunity you will ever have to dance. Dance with freedom and joy. Make some noise, if you feel so inclined. *Now, Lyla Rain wants to know...don't you feel better?*

> *~Now there's nothing left but to keep dancing.*
> *Author Unknown~*

32.   I Love You Exactly as You Are

One of my greatest joys is facilitating girls' self-esteem circles. We pass around a talking stick...a tradition borrowed from Native American teachers and healers. Whoever has the stick, in our case we use an agate heart, gets a turn to speak without interruption while the other girls give the best gift in the whole wide world...their gift of listening.

This circle is focused on helping the girls develop rock solid self-esteem and as part of the curriculum, I give the girls homework, or heart work, as I prefer to call it. The heart work is meant to be a tool to more deeply ground our topic and hopefully encourage their parents to join them in doing a ritual.

I hand each girl a piece of paper to take home with their heart work written on it. Today's was "Put your hand on your heart and tell yourself, I love you exactly as you are." Since I do the heart work with the girls, I put my piece of paper on the kitchen table. Every time I encounter it, I place my hand over my heart, take a deep breath, connect in with myself, and feel love for little ole me. I don't do anything to deserve the love, I feel it just because. The more I stop and say those words and feel that feeling, the more I feel love for me...just because I am me. It is powerful, nurturing heart work.

SOUL FULL self care

Write the words *"Put your hand on your heart and tell yourself I love you exactly as you are"* on a piece of paper. Every time you see that piece of paper, do it! Take a few deep breaths to ground yourself and feeeel gratitude and love for little ole you. Feel love for yourself exactly as you are.

That doesn't mean you will never stop growing or changing. It means that right now is enough. Take as long as you want or need to experience the nurturing of the present moment.

~In order to experience the magic of life, we must banish the doubt. Carlos Castenada~

33.   Light One Candle

The ceremonial use of lights has been used for thousands, perhaps millions of years. Lighting a candle is a simple practice found in many spiritual traditions around the globe.

Candles are common in worship places and are used to make ordinary space and/or time sacred. Often the flame is seen as a sign of the presence of God.

One single flame also stands for the unity that underlies all the traditions.

SOUL FULL self care

To practice, begin or end your day with the ritual of lighting a candle.

Make a special space where you are going to put one candle. It could be an altar or a shelf...a top of your dresser or a table. Make it pretty. If you don't have the time or inclination, then skip this step.

Light one candle to symbolize something especially for you. Perhaps, it represents your gratitude for this day, as an act of love toward yourself, as a prayer for peace, as a symbol of the strength available to you, or as a sign of your deep gratitude
for any of the blessings of life.

Sit for a moment or two as you think and feel what your candle symbolizes and celebrates.

You can also light a candle as a way of practicing "one-pointed attention." Sit comfortably and focus on the flame of the candle. If your attention wanders, gently bring your attention back to looking at the light.

~Dreams are candles to help us through the dark.
Once used, they have to melt.
Author Unknown~

34.   A Random Act of Kindness

We were a young family, and it was Mother's Day. We went out to a restaurant to celebrate. I was a bit anxious about spending money on eating out. I was a stay-at-home mom, and my partner's salary was supporting us. Eating at a restaurant was an enormous splurge for us. I didn't order the food I really wanted, I ordered what I thought was reasonable, and what we could afford. My children had made cards for me, and we had a wonderful time together.

When it was time to pay our check, the cashier told us that someone else paid for us and wished me a Happy Mother's Day. I was so shocked! Never, ever had I received such a generous anonymous gift! Not only did it make my day, it made me so happy to think about how good the person who paid must have felt.

Fast forward a few decades. My husband Bill and I were eating out. An elderly couple was at another table, and the man reminded us of Bill's dad who had recently died. I could feel my heart beating faster as I suggested we pay for their dinner. Bill was on board...we were pleased to have enough money to do this act of kindness.

We told the waiter our plan, and we were elated watching the shock and delight of the couple as they found out their bill had been paid. We felt great, they felt great, and when we were ready to leave, the waiter told us that we had made his day.

The owner opened the door for us as we left and thanked us for our generosity.

It seemed that our simple act of kindness had impacted quite a few folks.

Do something kind for someone today. Those who know and love you don't even need to know about this. You're not being kind to get a raise, to get acknowledgement, to get ahead. You are being kind just to practice being kind!

Generosity feels so good! You could open a door for someone whose arms are filled with groceries... let a mom with children go in front of you at the supermarket...pay someone's toll, wash someone's windshield at the gas station... give a lollipop to a child...buy a friend a cup of coffee...the ideas are endless.

This idea was inspired by the bumper sticker: Practice Random Acts of Kindness

~How wonderful it is that nobody need wait a single moment before starting to improve the world. Anne Frank~

35.   Prayerful Offering

No matter what our spiritual beliefs, most of us believe in a Higher Power: a Source, Divine creation, God, Goddess, some unnamable being. Throughout the ages, cultures all around the world have offered words of love and care, words requesting comfort and peace, and words of joy and praise to this creator of all things.

Every once in a while, when we call out in prayer, we realize that our physical world is but a fragment of the whole picture, a tiny piece of the puzzle. When we call out in prayer, the *small self* is reaching out to something greater. In those moments it realizes that it is but a drop of water from the bottomless sea.

SOUL FULL self care

Find a quiet place where you can have time to yourself - one minute, five minutes, any amount of time will do.

Fold your hands in a prayerful position at the center of your chest at your heart chakra. Now, offer up a prayer. Speak aloud whatever it is in your heart that wants to be said. Remember, you can't get this wrong. There is no one way to pray.

Feel your connection with all of the people over all of the years who have placed their palms together and offered up their own prayers. Feel a connection to yourself. Celebrate this moment.

~The stuff of our lives doesn't change. It is we who change in relation to it. Molly Vaas~

SOUL FULL self care

Think kind thoughts about yourself often
Greet the sun...feel the wonder of a brand new day
Girlfriend, take your bra off while you're at home
Take slow, deep breaths when you need soothing
Rub your own head, toes, feet, hands, arms
Walk barefoot as much as possible
Smile because you are alive
Doodle
Light a candle
Hug yourself often
Sit or lie on the earth.
Laugh because it feels good
Breathe deeply into your belly
Sit quietly for a few moments
Wear pajamas for the whole day
Have a picnic dinner on your bed
Pray for those with less than you
Bathe in gratitude at the end of the day
Go for a walk even though your list isn't done
HarmonyRoseWellness.com

Review

If you feel that this book has added value to the quality of your life, I would love for you to take a few minutes to leave an honest review on Amazon. Your feedback helps others decide if this book will support them in living their best life.

All the best, Harmony Rose West

HarmonyRoseWellness.com

Printed in Great Britain
by Amazon

21360128R00045